To Know Me

Gillian Mairi Bailey

Black Eyes Publishing UK

To Know Me
By Gillian Mairi Bailey
© Gillian Mairi Bailey 1970-2014, 2019

Published by Black Eyes Publishing UK. 2019
Brockworth, Gloucestershire, England
www.blackeyespublishinguk.co.uk

ISBN: 978-1-913195-01-4

A CIP catalogue record for this title is available from the British Library.

Cover Template: Jason Conway, cre8urbrand.
                     www.cre8urbrand.co.uk

Gillian Mairi Bailey
1935 - 2014

To Mum,

who showed us the poetry, in life.

Contents

Appendices

Introduction

Gillian Mairi Bailey was born in Haverhill, Suffolk in 1935.

From her early school years words illuminated her path. In her prose piece entitled, 'Five Good Things About Me' she recalls the process of learning to read, as words hanging 'in front of me like a string of bright raindrops.' The realisation dawned on her, 'I can do anything, know everything. I can read.'

Gillian gained a first-class English degree at Leeds University, before meeting and marrying the Reverend John Bailey. They travelled to Australia on missionary work with their young son, Mark, and returned several years later, when Gillian was pregnant with her daughter. Subsequently she taught English at a secondary school, sharing her love of language. Later her strong social conscience led her into becoming a member of the Labour Party, as well as protesting at Greenham Common. By the mid 1970's she'd switched her focus to enabling refugees and migrants to learn English and find employment. This role filled the next twenty years of her life until she retired.

At last having time to develop a voice of her own, Gillian enrolled in an Open Studies poetry course, achieving another first. She became heavily influenced by the First World War poets, as well as other contemporary female poets, and it is during this period that Gillian wrote the majority of her work, presented here in 'To Know Me'. She also became co-editor of a local poetry magazine, entitled 'WordPlay'. It is probable that she submitted her work to various publications and won several awards, but unfortunately, details of these accomplishments are missing.

Gillian was diagnosed with Parkinson's in 1997. Sadly, the rapid progress of this disease severely curtailed her ability to write, and dried up a well of verse still untapped. Yet her love for poetry never left her. She remained able to quote and recognise any number of poets. She died in 2014.

In March 2019, during a chance conversation with Katy Bailey, we learned of her mother's poetry, and the fact that, Gillian Mairi Bailey had never been published. We asked to see some examples of her work and were immediately impressed by their quality. We suggested a book of nineteen poems, along with five prose pieces.

However, Josephine Lay, 'Black Eyes' creative writing adviser, and a poet herself, realized that Gillian's poetic voice lay barely hidden within two of her prose pieces. By teasing out 'found words and phrases' Josephine was able to create two additional poems, almost entirely out of Gillian's own words. These have now been included to make total of twenty-one poems.

Black Eyes Publishing UK

To Know Me

Blackberry Jam

I calendar the season
before the devil spits.
Do not follow Country Code
but hack and hook and claw;
an aged Sebastian
freckled veins cross-hatched.

Scourged with nettles,
pierced with thorns,
I tunnel thickets,
mine enclosures
where seed heads rattle
on barren soil.

Lush clusters droop
like glaucous jet
enamelled flies bloat
on them, are husked
in clammy webs. My bag
billows with the seething fruit.

In man's frail season,
bait my winter shelves.
Practised eyes coax
from Puritan jars.
Waxed paper circles
seal wise women's guile

'Plant of Venus in House of Mars'

Sheltered Living

We fold the sheet:
perform
the ritual
pavane:
forward, join,
a quarter turn
and back.
My fingers fumble.
Yours are sure.

At home, your sheets
were stacked
on cleanly shelves;
and smelled of air
and bonfires.

'Cabined and confined'
Old woman's clothes
(your own or previous
occupant's?) look
pinched in oak veneer;
pastel arms
signaling distress
protrude
from linen white-out.

Forward, back
and fold
The final figure
before
the sheet is stowed.

Men's Changing Room

We seek the juvenescence
of our joints, our juices;
to sublimate sciatica,
subdue cholesterol.
Would we be here without
the exhortations of our wives?
Swimming up and down
is boring.

We smooth cream
into our withered parts,
our shrunken hearts,
where, still, illusion swells;
and recognize that younger men
are more endowed.

Veloured in leisure suits
we spin lost odysseys.
(The sail-filled Cyclades
solicit us no more).
We order coffee
from a dark, Italian girl
whose eyes are heavy
with her nights of joy.

We burn for her
to notice us. "Due cappuccino,
per favore," we entreat her.
*(Oh, give me your answer,
or else I will die).*
She smiles, like a madonna,
and brims the cups with foam.

Peacock Hunting Butterflies at Charlecote Park

Sultan of spikenard
I swirl through minarets in bloom:
flush out pretenders –
the Peacock-winged;
Red Admirals; Tortoiseshells:
all infidels.

Observe
the curved precision of my beak:
they are impaled:
enter my Paradise.

At dusk when violet skies
are pierced with stars,
my wives in burkas
lead me to my bower,
and there I woo my chosen one
with a raga of shrill cries.

Their plangent sounds
ruffle the moon-struck deer who brood
beyond the perfumed gardens,
in Nawab's grounds.

Collective Memory

Springtime and flat fields fold
into the Channel. Coaches trawl
the highways. Reconnoitre
salient, Ypres and Mons.
No speck of green or farm
outbuilding only the yellow
clay and standing water.

Our coaches park in gabled
squares, by gaunt cathedrals
where the walls are lined
with the names of soldiers
rank on rank. Only
their Colours fade and fray
like uniforms 'sent home'.

I think I saw in fresh turned fields
the hands of dead men
half obscured with loam,
grasping at air. No need
of bodies in this death affair
only the age-old exegesis
'Lost in Battle,' stays.

Caedmon

In his sleep, he remembered water splashing
and tumbling from gullies drenched
with ferns; but the words to describe it lay,
like toads, in his mouth and he could not utter.

When he drove the cows to pasture,
the hedgerows were slanted with purslane
and bluebells, stitchwort and buttercups,
so that the path he trod was a prism;

but the words to describe it teemed, like fish,
in his mouth and would not leap out.
He longed to magnify Creation
in flawless plainsong;

then annotate margins
with the cream and sorrel gradations
of a butterfly
lodged in the tracery of an arch.

When only motes stirred in thin air,
Caedmon woke in the straw and heard
words clamouring inside living rock.
He set them free like grace-notes.

Tongue untied.

The Lifeless Leaf

In spring
as green as grass
beautiful
as the tree itself.

A leaf
so brown and cobwebbed;
jagged and tattered.
A leaf
with no life in it.
Like thread
made into a pattern;

So that's
how the leaf looks
to me.

Exile – A Story of Great Distances

They arrived, disparate
in all but Exile.
Quiescent, nurturing
regrowth of strength.
How cruel we were,
'No smoking. Do not spit
or clear the throat of prison phlegm.'

They gave no hostages.
Did not tell of limbs
arthritic from the rack;
blindfolded eyes;
and the sly delvings
into hidden parts.
We taught them English.

In time they showed us
photographs;
a Graduation; snow
on incandescent mountains.
In time, remembered songs
of liberation. Danced.
Had rows with past confreres.

We found them jobs
as warehouse porters;
care assistants; cleaners
in intellectual's houses.
They endured 'emergency
accommodation', but forced
their children on to better things.

A military Dictator
is made a Senator for life.
Exchange past wrongs
for hint of liberties regained.

We do so in your names;
but we have never trekked
the distances in exile.

The Police Named Him 'Adam'
(On the torso of a child found floating in the Thames)

Little bag of bones caught
in a cross current, your head
and limbs are severed:
reed beds close over them.
Later, washed up on the river bank
seven candles and a white sheet;
perhaps, your name written on them.

Adekoye Jo
Fola Adeoye

Little body let
your tongue and the half
moons of your nails;
your boneless, baby knees
and the dappled reaches
of your skull sing together.
Let those bones live

to *re*-call the broken
bodies of children:
to *re*-member them.

Previously Published in Wordplay Pamphlet, Volume 3, Summer 2003

Police investigating the "ritualistic" killing of a young boy whose torso was found in the Thames, on 21st September 2001, have ruled out any links to candles and a sheet also found in the river.

Scotland Yard officers had investigated links between the killing and the items which had a man's name written on them.

Detectives have now eliminated the clues after a man was interviewed in New York and gave reasons for why they were found in the Thames.

The boy's killing is believed to be the first "Muti" killing in the UK, a human sacrifice which is practiced in southern Africa.

BBC News, 14th February 2002

By a Stained-Glass Window in the Chapel
(On the Demolition of Central Hospital, Warwickshire)

What scene of devastation
below me now I see.
I view the desolation
brought by the JCB.

My hooker green, my crimson
are scarred with ghastly stars.
The vandals sell my leading
to Birmingham scrap yards.

My day of consecration
how glorious was I then.
The choir and congregation,
the Mayor and aldermen.

Asylum for the County.
How modern and how kind.
Peace for the weary bodies.
Hope for the troubled mind.

Financial fluctuations.
No money left to spare.
Abolish institutions.
Community must care.

And round me ever vaster
an Executive Estate.
The rich still in their castle.
The poor still at the gate.

Both shining ones and lowly
God grant you grace that ye
do not requite your future
in a rented B and B

Remember, 'One in Three.'

Central Hospital was a psychiatric hospital located in Hatton, Warwickshire, England, between 1852 and 1995.

Formerly known as Warwick County Lunatic Asylum it was renamed and integrated into the newly formed National Health Service in 1948.

'The sun shall not strike thee by day, nor the moon by night'
Psalm 121:6, The Bible

The Woman Who Loved Opera

'One fine day…' my mother
sang. *Basso profundo,*
as she swept the stairs
with worn down bristles
and a freckled pan. Housework
was a personal affront to her.

She remembered when
she had dazzled in Derby
at the Metropole Hotel
and been wooed by
the younger sons
of worsted millionaires.

Gentled by Opera she snuffed
hallowed names; Gigli
at the Empire: Mimi and her tiny
frozen hand. Slowly, by osmosis,
we absorbed her lore, mined treasure
which we did not know we had.

And so, we swelled from Gods
to Balcony, from stalls to box,
until my brother, her Rodolfo,
died. Estranged by grief,
a wounded animal who clawed,
she mourned his loss alone.

Hardly waiting for me to leave.
She played the tapes he'd copied
for her and said she's heard his voice,
just at the change. One winter day
she fell where frost filled
bruised blue hollows by the door.

At her funeral in the red brick
Crematorium we played
'Mimi' and 'One Fine Day'
and wept which she
would never have allowed.

The '£10 Englishmen' Return to Cape York

By ten-pound passage sealed,
we sailed where mangroves
comb lagoons; where rollers
fold on shoreline scrolled
with colonnades of palms.
Endeavour flapped becalmed
upon that ocean's jade cuirass;
and Cook claimed *Terra Nullius*
for an unknown Crown.

We lived in villages on stilts
in gouged earth clearings
by the quivering Bush.
Women wore corollas
of hibiscus in their hair;
and little children clung
to butterflies, as big as plates,
on tree binds strung.

We circumnavigate the rim
of forty years; careen
on four-wheel drive past
termite Guardians signing
magnetic north. We stand
upon the armoured snout
of our lost continent. Find
deeps where currents interlock
and luggers plunge in spindrift.

Market Town / New Airport

In Spring, this outpost of airport
recalls its provenance. It rides
the broad backs of a flock of hills
under a sky speckled with birdsong.
In espaliered gardens, new wood
is auburn or tasseled with saffron.
Palladian villas promenade
the Market's ravished square.

A river slides between blind walls.
It swirls by sidings where the trucks
are linked with bindweed;
chokes on honeycombs
of polystyrene; clutches
at broken spars from pallets.
Gulls pick and stab
on mud flats skeined with prints.

Above scorched fields and loops
of motorways, planes,
like condors, soar
through chartered skies.
But magnolias still
curve their waxen tips,
and plumes of cherry blossom
brush intensity of blue.

So, do not count me out of this.

For H. W.

He died last week respected,
as they say, by all who knew him.
A simple man who followed City.
Regularly attended Lords.

At fifteen was the office junior:
At fifty, chairman of the board.
His face was seen on television,
predicting base rate's rise and fall.

A frequent luncher at the Palace;
innocently pleasured by success.
And yet a gentle man who tended
a gentle wife for ten rich years.

And after,
Made mince pies,
At Christmas
Just as 'once she had'.

Comfortable in death,
a chieftain in his place.
Go forward, Neighbour,
exemplar of grace.

Kings College Chapel

In this nave, masons
entranced by light fanned
stone ribs into vaulting;
they trellised it with emblems.

Windows bloom on us.
We inhabit their Eden:
wear blue without stain of sin
and Eve's terra cotta.

Outside, light drenches air.
Reflections swirl
in teal-green reservoirs
where willows dip their weeds.

My grey face
appals
in the car mirror
when I was cast out.

But I keep hidden
an ivory boat.
Spars and rigging
tensile as the Dove returning.

Bananas

Bananas were exiled from us
by the war and somehow seemed
a fabulous fruit, nether here
nor there. 'Yes, we have no
bananas. We have no
bananas today.' We sang,
and felt deprived.

We knew about them
from our schoolbooks.
They grew in hands which looked
like boxing gloves with fingers
or the friendly pads of apes.
We crayoned them custard yellow;
waited for the War to end.

They travelled steerage
and arrived sallow and briny
from the hold. They became
a gauge of moral rectitude
'Bananas should be eaten shared.'
Against gluttony, 'A boy
ate six and died.'

Their calypso glamour dimmed.
They were hybridized;
forced to endure a culinary
status no other fruit would stand for:
Nesquik and Banoffee Pie;
ersatz flavouring which blew
the bony chambers of the skull.

But I remember how I used to lie
on my veranda. My harvest hung
in hands above my head like
shifting coral. I would take each fruit

and taste the just-set fullness
of its curds; cool as the winds that blow
through colonnades of palms
by oceans lapped with cream.
My first Eden.

The line,

'Yes, we have no
bananas. We have no
bananas today.'

From 'Yes! We Have No Bananas',
a novelty song by Frank Silver and Irving Cohn.
Originally published 19th July 1923.
Entered the Public Domain 1st January 2019.

Surrounded by Cornfields *

Surrounded by cornfields,
rolling prairies pressed against a garden fence
traversed by footpaths – a farmer's breadth - which led
to a low horizon and a sky made colourless by heat.
One meadow survived - the school playing field
mown twice a year - we burrowed in its hay
revelling in warmth and the smell of motor oil.

We were stolid children
living in deep countryside - the school field
provided our folk lore. We named its flora,
devised its rituals. The field was a sea of
waving grasses interspersed with taller flowers:
satin skirted poppies, cornflowers
and white ox-eye daisies.

Beneath - an enameled
setting of scarlet pimpernels, speedwell,
campanula and bird's foot trefoil.
We sucked honey from white and purple deadnettle's
rolled our tongues around the astringent
savour of field sorrel. We dipped chins into
buttercup goblets to see if we liked butter.

In April or early May,
we abandoned the field for forays
into Wilsey Woods to gather peggles, where
bluebells drifted in a purple haze over glass green
stalks and leaves - there was always a frisson of unease.
We were frightened of the stoats and weasels
when we heard the drawn-out scream of a rabbit.

Then there was
the dreadful Keeper's larder, a rank odour,
among the bluebells, where carcasses of
predators were strung up to deter others. And

Old Velvet, a cadaverous figure dressed in black,
who wandered the woods obsessively rubbing
a piece of velvet between his dirt freckled fingers.

As we grew older
the field became a centre for assignations.
Couples would rise as one from the long grass.
If we met now, we would remember the glories
of that ordinary Suffolk field; share daisy heads
on plaited grass plates and return in the shadow-less
evenings of double summertime to our first homes.

*

*Josephine Lay formed this poem from Gillian's prose piece 'The School
Field' using nothing but Gillian's own words. See introduction.*

The Fox and the Wardrobe*

On top of the wardrobe was a fox.
Not a jolly kind of fox in houndstooth check
and knee-breeches, but a sly, feral creature
lurking behind the hat boxes ready to leap out
and strike with his yellowed incisors
should a child be unwise enough
to be alone in the room, in the dark.

The wardrobe had a shiny, oak veneer;
it was my mother's, where she kept her
frocks, coats, skirts and her fox fur.
My parents retained a raffish whiff
of the Thirties; he in his plus-fours,
she in black coat and skirt, a stiffened,
felt oval perched diagonally on her
'Marcelled' head. The fox fur snuggled
triumphantly around her powdered neck,
gazing sycophantically at her cupid bow lips.

I knew that fox. Absurd to say it but
I was jealous. I felt plain, shy and
rather boring in my parents' eyes.
A disappointment. One afternoon
I determined to settle the conflict between us.
The fox lay curled in its usual position
with its snout overhanging the edge of the
wardrobe and its wicked orange eyes
fixed intently on my throat. I placed
the back of a chair against the wardrobe door.

Holding a scarf with which to muffle the fox,
I being unable to handle its bony skull
or impenetrable fur, I made a grab
for its body. The chair tilted,
slid inexorably down the shiny veneer.
Its passing left a gaping wound

the length of the door. My parents
found me lying on the carpet,
hat boxes around me and the fox's fur
sodden with my tears, suffocating my mouth.
The wound on the wardrobe door
stood revealed in all its savagery.

The fox and the wound remained.
The fox observed my father's death
and the wound, pale ivory by now,
was still there as the undertakers
removed his body, with a final scratch
as the bier grazed the door.

My mother still slept in the same room
with the dust settling like snow drifts
on the surfaces of the furniture. The fox
too slept on, a grey ghost half submerged
in old tights, and peeling suitcases. Then,
quite suddenly, my mother died. Her children
gathered to clear the house.

The wardrobe went to a rehabilitation project.
It fell to me to remove the fox. We lit a bonfire
in the garden under the apple trees.
I carried the fox out, still muffled in cloth,
I shook it free into the flames.
It burned fiercely with a tang of singed fur
the backing curled into an oily tendril
like the charred backbone of a snake.
I stamped out the embers,
one fiery eye remained,
reminding me that all things pass.

*

*Josephine Lay formed this poem from Gillian's prose piece 'The Fox Fur
and The Wardrobe' using mostly Gillian's own words. See introduction.*

To the Editor, 'The Times', London, from his Commissioner in the Highlands

Glencalvie, Spring, 1845.
Sir, as commissioned, I present
my observations viz
the recent Clearances in Ross-Shire.

An intemperate season......

the waters fitful amethyst
and the braes russet to umber,
sage to burning ochre
merging and muted
in the slanting rain.

I MET THE CLANS FOLK ON A BRAESIDE
by the Carron. The women seemly
in netted caps and shawls: the men
wrapped in their shepherd's plaids.
They spoke, in their own tongue, the Psalm,
'The eyes of all things wait on thee.
The Giver of all good.' Their voices
rose and fell, harsh in the high air
and scattered with the hail.

THE HILLSIDE WATCHED THEM
as their column wound out of the glen.
(Only Hugh Ross remained but he
Lay dying). They carried with them nothing
but their bedding and little children slung
like incubi around their sibling' necks.
Croick graveyard furnished shelter
of a sort: four stone walls, a few bent trees,
familial headstones marking off
dead years; the unpleasant cough of sheep.

WITHIN TWO DAYS AN AIMLESS MOVING ON
They could not hear the air unsettled
by the grief of children nor the wind soughing
through the famished grass. In bitterness
of spirit scratched their shame upon
the window of Croick church, *'Glencalvie*
people, the wicket generation.'

'CLENCALVIE IS A WILDERNESS
BLOW SHIP THEM TO THE COLONY.'

John Ross, shepherd, tarried here.

Julian of Norwich (1342 – after 1416)

I am Julian, denizen
of Norfolk where
sails like fading petals
traverse salt marshes;
and air is bounded
with birdsong.

I am Julian
not given to excess,
an anchorite
within the wall
of Saint Julian's
church in Norwich.

My cell is dry
and cool like the brush
of fingertips;
sound and sweet
as a hazelnut cupped
in the palm of my hand.

I am Julian
short on theology,
only remembering
sixteen 'shewings'
on one day in one year
and thereafter meditating.

For twenty years
He sheweth, keepeth, loveth.
Knowing my provenance
He me endows
with solace in solitude
as my soul requires.

Playground Rules

One too many for him;
he hunches and shakes his head.

Too dumb to fight;
his fingers hang like lumps of lard
beneath unravelling sleeves.

He rubs his knuckles over smarting eyes;
his piggy features puff and flame.

Don't come near – unless you want the same.

Appendices

Five Good Things about Me

We are sitting on the splintery floor in our classroom. Our Beacon Readers are in front of us. Mrs. Beer is holding up flash cards. She points to one and says, 'dog d-o-g'. We point to the word in our Reader and say, 'd-o-g dog'. Am I pointing to the right word? I don't know. To me each word is a picture. I can see a dog. A friendly black and white dog with a lolling red tongue and clever eyes; but it isn't on the page. He's jumping all over me. 'Take me for a walk,' he says. In the book he's called Mr. Dan. He's Old Lob's sheep dog. We should all be like him: Kind. Helpful. Honest. And Cou-rt-e-ous.

I do not like Mrs. Beer. She shouts. She doesn't want to be here. My mother says it's because she's deaf. I think it's because of the war. All the lady teachers who are not married have gone to fight Hitler. Mrs. Beer is holding up another card, 'Who can tell me what this word says?' she asks.

I look at the word. It is not a picture. It is not an animal or even a table. 'C-o-u-l-d. C-o-u-l-d, Could.' I know what it says.
I shoot up my hand. Mrs. Beer looks annoyed. 'It says could'.
'It says could', I cry with complete and utter certainty; and suddenly all the other words fall into place. They hang in front of me like a string of bright raindrops. I can do anything. I can know everything. I can read.

Mrs. Beer would have derived a certain satisfaction when her predictions that my dreaminess would be the ruin of any future career were at first realized. Having sworn that I would never be a teacher I found myself entering the profession ingloriously by the back door, at that time one could teach without a certificate as long as one had a degree. But she would also have been surprised to learn that not only did I like teaching; I was good at it.

I cherish certain incidents, icons even, that tell me I must have done something right. My life has been caught up in sociological changes of the century. People flowed out of Britain as well as flowing in. We paid our £10 passage and emigrated to Australia. I was to be Government Teacher in a tin hut with a sand floor set amongst the Bush in the far north of Cape York. I remember one morning of overwhelming joy when the children of Cowell Creek, three miles walk through the bush, brought me armfuls of yellow wattle flowers and I was instantly transported to Leeds in the early spring when mimosa blossom was reflected in the rainy pavements outside the flower shops and its fragrance lingered in the sooty air.

When we returned to England, I found myself teaching the waves of refugees and migrants who flocked to Coventry. I remember Ahmed, part time Imam at the Mosque, who engaged the local Priest in the church hall where we held our classes in a theological disputation on the nature of the Trinity. Neither held it against the other and Ahmed would slap the Priest on the back and chant 'is a mystery, is a mystery'. I felt enormously honoured when I heard him telling a new student, 'Gillian's alright. She's… sensible'.

Many of the Punjabi students were illiterate in their own language and they used to roll around on the floor helpless with laughter when we enacted dramas about visiting the Doctor. 'Doctor I have a pain in my belly button.' To cross them would have been like crossing the assembled ranks of the Women's Institute so I was relieved to hear their leader remark, 'Julien I like she.'

Now I am older I hold these memories to me as charms against the dark. The most miraculous of all was when I saw my first grandchild for the first time. She was golden from head to toe, swathed in a cocoon of clothing like a beautiful golden grub. My reason told me she was jaundiced but her downy hair covered her head with a goldsmith's finest filigree. I found myself thinking, 'this child is mine.' Not in any possessive manner but in the love, I felt for my daughter and through her for the developing life of this infant. 'Love set you going like a fat gold watch'.

The School Field

We were surrounded by cornfields. Rolling prairies pressed against a garden fence, traversed only by footpaths, a farmer's breadth, which led to a low horizon and a sky made colourless by heat.

One meadow survived because it was the School playing field. It was known prosaically by that name and was mown twice a year. We burrowed in its hay revelling in warmth and the smell of motor oil.

We were stolid children living in deep countryside and not given to excess, determinedly resisting any attempts by our teachers to persuade us to go a'maying or indulge in Maypole Dancing. The school field and its environs provided our folk lore. We named its flora and devised its rituals.

For much of the year the field was a sea of waving grasses interspersed with taller flowers: satin skirted poppies, cornflowers and white ox-eye daisies. Beneath these was an enamelled setting of Scarlet Pimpernel, Speedwell, the colour of English eyes, delicate bell-shaped Campanula and Bird's Foot Trefoil with its plump yolk coloured petals and their golden brown stridations which we called 'bacon and eggs'.

We sucked the honey from the receptacles of white and purple Deadnettles and rolled our tongues around the astringent savour of Field Sorrel. We dipped chins into Buttercup goblets to see if we liked butter. We drew fierce moustachios on our faces with the powder which came from Blackgrass and, at a very tender age, we were initiated by the big girls into a game called 'cocks and hens' which involved the anatomical sexing of grasses.

In late Aril and early May, we abandoned the field to go on forays to Wilsey Woods to gather Peggles and Bluebells. (These subsequently wilted in jam jars on the Nature Table). Peggles were like Cowslips but with Primrose-shaped flowers. Their petals were as mild and wholesome as a pitcher of cream. In another part of the woods Bluebells drifted in a purple haze over their glass green stalks and leaves. But there was always a certain frisson of unease. We were frightened of the stoats and weasels and knew what was happening when we heard the drawn-out scream of a rabbit. Then there was the dreadful Keeper's Larder, a rank odour among the Bluebells, where the carcasses of predators were strung up to deter the others. Worst of all was 'Old Velvet' a cadaverous figure dressed in black, who wandered the woods obsessively rubbing a piece of velvet between his dirt freckled fingers.

As we grew older the field became a centre for assignations where couples would rise as one from the long grass when they heard the village policeman approach. A consequence of such activity was that the village florist would be asked to make up an extra-large bouquet as cover for some unwilling bride as she made her progress down the church aisle.

I puzzled over the desertion of my friends and wondered what quality they had which boys found lacking in me. But the democracy of the field was over. That great leveler the 11+ had destined me for the Grammar School and them for work at fourteen. But I like to think that if we met now, we would remember the glories of that ordinary Suffolk field; share daisy heads on plaited grass plates and return in the shadow-less evenings of Double Summertime to our first homes.

'Call for me tomorrow.'

'Yes, I'll call for you tomorrow. My Confrere.'

The Fox Fur and the Wardrobe

Just after 1932 when they got married, my parents won £500 on the football pools and prepared to furnish their new house with it. They bought a dining room suite and velvet cushioned armchairs and a settee for the lounge. The bought a kitchenette and a looming giant refrigerator; and a glass-topped dressing table and two wardrobes in shiny oak veneer for the principal bedroom. The larger of the two was my mother's where she kept all her frocks and coats and skirts.

On top of the wardrobe was a fox. Not a jolly anthropomorphic kind of fox in a houndstooth check shirt and knee-breeches but a sly feral creature lurking behind the hat boxes ready to leap out and strike with his yellowed incisors should a child be unwise enough to be alone in the room - in the dark – with him.

My parents always retained a raffish whiff of the Thirties. He in his plus-fours in the Lounge Bar of the Clubhouse. She in black coat and skirt, a stiffened felt oval perched diagonally on her Marcelled head; and of course, the fox fur snuggled triumphantly around her powdered neck, gazing sycophantically at her rouged cheeks and cupid bow lips. I knew that fox. Absurd to say it but I was jealous. I felt plain and shy and rather boring in my parents' eyes. A disappointment.

One afternoon I determined to settle the conflict between us once and for all. The fox lay curled up in its usual position with its snout overhanging the edge of the wardrobe and its wicked orange eyes fixed intently on my throat. I placed the back of the chair against the wardrobe door and holding a large scarf with which I untended to muffle the fox, it being beyond me to handle its bony skull or impenetrable fur, made a grab for its body. The chair tilted on its back legs and slid inexorably down the shiny veneer. Its passing left a gaping wound the whole length of the door.

My parents found me lying on the carpet, hat boxes all around me and the fox's fur sodden with my tears half suffocating my mouth and nose. The wound on the wardrobe door stood revealed in all its savagery.

The years passed and the fox and the wound remained. The fox observed my father's death and the wound, pale ivory by now, was still there as the undertakers removed his body with a final scratch as the bier grazed the door.

My mother still slept in the same bedroom with the dust settling like snow drifts on the surfaces of the furniture. The fox too slept on, a grey ghost half submerged in old tights, birthday cards and empty peeling suitcases. Then, quite suddenly, my mother died and her children gathered to clear the house. The wardrobe went to a rehabilitation project for young offenders. It fell to me to remove the fox. We lit a bonfire in the garden under the apple trees. I carried the fox out still muffled in a cloth. I shook it free into the hear of the flames. They burned fiercely. There was a smell of singed fur and then the backing curled into an oily tendril almost like the charred backbone of a snake. I stamped out the embers. One remaining fiery eye reminded me that all things pass.

A Duet with Dame Myra

My bedroom was at the front of the house and was shaped like the viewing deck of an Ocean-going Liner. In winter I lay in bed and saw the sun ascending as a fiery pillar into a high clear sky. Bare branches were silhouetted against white fields; the privet hedge next to the path spider-webbed with diamonds. I could hear the click clack of my spaniel's feathered paws and his ritual barking as the postman approached the gate.

It was two years after the war had ended but my room still retained the almost deliberate shabbiness which characterized my mother's approach to housekeeping. Condensation froze to ice on the unpainted metal frames of the windows and the threadbare carpet was worn down in places to the canvas. My bed was heaped with yellow blankets edged with unraveled blanket stitch.

How intolerant I was then. There came a time when I could scarcely bear to be with my parents in the evenings. Tea eaten, homework done, I would announce that I was going to bed. My bedroom was my fortress. I lay in bed and went over the events of the day; small triumphs won, splendours seen, myself as the constant centre of my dramas. Sex concerned me very little, being much addicted to the 'Anne of Green Gables' stories where Anne and her chum Diana, who looked like a moss rose, were pure examples of Canadian girlhood and Anne with her wide grey eyes and auburn hair transfixed her friends with anthropomorphic tales of silver birches and placid lakes.

My mother tried, 'Girls of your age don't go to bed at eight o'clock. Why don't you join something?'
Me, 'What?'
'The church youth club? You might meet some nice people there.'
I knew she meant boys, 'I despise the youth club'
'It's up to you, Madam, and take that look off your face. I've tried my best. No one's good enough for you.'

She hated being pitied by the vicar who knew that all the other mother's daughters had boyfriends. To compensate for my lack of charms my mother invented more esoteric accomplishments for me. I had recently been constrained to learn the piano and was taught by a timid lady named Miss Nunn who had plaits of mouse brown hair wound around her ears like earmuffs. Both Miss Nunn and I knew that I would never master the left hand but she needed the money and I enjoyed coming home alone in the semi-darkness, the metal clegs on my shoes striking sparks from the icy pavements, knowing that if I just moved my feet a little bit faster I would take off and fly. It was like riding a bicycle. Meanwhile I let it be understood that I was 'gifted' at the piano and had attracted the attention of several distinguished artistes.

During and just after the war the Arts Council had been set up to bring culture to communities who were deprived of it by reasons of transport and security. The Organizer in our area was Mrs. Hall who was the wife of the Relief Stationmaster on the Haverhill to Cambridge line. Whenever I think of Mrs. Hall, I understand why her son Peter became a theatre impresario. Indefatigable in rayon silk two pieces, her little current eyes gleaming with missionary fervour, she was on first name terms with such shining ones as Benjamin Britten and Dame Myra Hess.

I knew from the triumphant expression on my mother's face when I came in from school that fatal day that something had happened. She slapped down a hunk of bread and jam and announced, 'Well, I've done it. I've had a word with Mrs. Hall at the Mother's Union and you're to meet Dame Myra Hess and maybe she'll give you a few tips. Play a piece with you,' One horrified moment of realization and I fled upstairs.
'Never mind that one. Don't know how to please her.'

My fortress was my fortress no longer. I had sinned. I had been guilty of pride and deception and I would be exposed. Mt protestations were useless. The event was embroidered to such an extent that it was reliably reported I was to play a duet with Dame Myra at the next Arts Council concert. I tossed and turned in bed each night so that even my mother got worried and I was taken to the Doctor who asked me about my periods and let his hand run accidentally down my leg. Of course, Mrs. Hall, as impressarios will, had forgotten her promise almost as soon as she had made it and my mother found other things to grumble about; but for may months I forwent fantasy and found consolation in Religion… instead.

Haverhill

I was born in Haverhill in 1935 and lived there until I was twenty. This was before the days of the Greater London Overspill when Haverhill grew in size if not in beauty, but Timpson's description of it as being in Victorian times 'a sort of rural Leeds.' Remained true in the 1950s. so much so that in the villages around one local wag would say to another,

'Where you'm going for your holidays, Bor?

'Going? Going like as heck. I'm a-going to 'Avril,' Haverhill being the rural equivalent of a weekend on Wigan Pier.

Al least four roads lead to Haverhill, each name denoting the cosmopolitian nature of the tribes who had come there and the passed through, leaving it a windy empty place smelling, when the wind was in the right quarter, of the sea which was not so far away by seagull flight. On boisterous windswept days when the clouds were tossed high into a water colour sky, seagulls covered the horse trough and drinking fountain in the centre of the town like a thick soft quilt. Their cries set the teeth on edge and these combined with the grit of a chalky dust made people quick and sharp and disinclined to linger.

To reach the fountain from the Withersfield Road where I was born one had in my opinion to pass some very interesting buildings. The first was the place where the dead people live – the Cemetery. This as neat and well-laid out as a Logo town. There was a squat red brick chapel with a pointed spire and near rows of headstones in a shiny brawn coloured stone. Each designated rectangle was filled with the marble chippings with which I weighed down my pockets. My parents were not from this area and so I had no family graves to visit but I longed, how I longed, to make the ritual visitation on a Sunday afternoon with my basket and my gardening gloves and my shears. I even contemplated bribing my school friends to allow me to go with them as a kind of surrogate grandchild.

There were two other places of religion before one reached the school. The first was a cream and green tin tabernacle where the Roman Catholics worshipped. It had unlikely Italianate windows which I used to creep up to try to glimpse inside. There was a red light and a gleam of silver and gold but then I was usually chased away by the priest who had an athletic turn of speed and a hard hand. There were few of his faith in Haverhill which was part of the diocese of Portsmouth, a hundred miles away! But to me it was the most romantic of beliefs. At that time, I was a recusant in religion and a Cavalier in politics as opposed to most of the townsfolk who were Liberals and Non-Conformists. Who knew what theological disputation had caused them to build the West End Chapel at one end of the town and the Old Independent Chapel at the other?

After the Old Independent one came to the school which was the true fount of our religious education. The headmistress was Miss Potter, Miss Potter was a member of the Peculiar Baptist Sect and was adept at inculcating a sense of sin from which I have never yet recovered. Above her desk was a large framed picture entitled, 'Jesus friend of little children.' Above the 'punishment cupboard' was a decorated text, 'Thou, God seeest me.' It was rumoured there was a cane inside the cupboard but it was never used. Miss Potter just talked very slowly and very sadly her large round eyes floating behind thick pebble glasses. One found oneself promising to be a better girl. An example to the little ones and a source of pride to one's parents.

In spite of these protestations a friend and I soon succumbed. There was a large schoolgirl in the Dandy comic called Pansy Potter. She too had round pebble glasses, the comparison was inevitable. It so happened we were wandering up Wratting Road to which we had recently moved. Literally, as well as metaphorically, a step upwards for it was hilly and the bank on either side supported by a stone wall. One of us picked up a piece of chalk; a round face with glasses was drawn on the wall and sub-titled 'Pansy Potter.'

The next day we were called into the Hall. The atmosphere was as doom-laden as when the school's pet rabbit had died. The perpetrator was urged to confess. Mention was made of the joy over one sinner who repenteth but if no one came forward the whole school would stay in... indefinitely.

We sat. In the end there was nothing they could do. Our sins had not found us out: but do not imagine we did not suffer the torments of the damned. Forgive us Miss Potter. We have tender consciences ever since.